The Key Facts™ on

Turkmenistan

Essential Information on Turkmenistan

By Patrick W. Nee

The Internationalist®

www.internationalist.com

The Internationalist®

International Business, Investment, and Travel

Published by:

The Internationalist Publishing Company

96 Walter Street/ Suite 200

Boston, MA 02131, USA

Tel: 617-354-7722

www.internationalist.com

PN@internationalist.com

Table Of Contents

Chapter 1: Background

Present-day Turkmenistan covers territory that has been at the crossroads of civilizations for centuries. The area was ruled in antiquity by various Persian empires, and was conquered by Alexander the Great, Muslim crusaders, the Mongols, Turkic warriors, and eventually the Russians. In medieval times Merv (today known as Mary) was one of the great cities of the Islamic world and an important stop on the Silk Road. Annexed by Russia in the late 1800s, Turkmenistan later figured prominently in the anti-Bolshevik movement in Central Asia. In 1924, Turkmenistan became a Soviet republic; it achieved independence upon the dissolution of the USSR in 1991. Extensive hydrocarbon/natural gas reserves, which have yet to be fully exploited, have begun to transform the country. Turkmenistan is moving to expand its extraction and delivery projects. The Government of Turkmenistan is actively working to diversify its gas export routes beyond the still important Russian pipeline network. In 2010, new gas export pipelines that carry Turkmen gas to China and to northern Iran began operating, effectively ending the Russian monopoly on Turkmen gas exports. President for Life Saparmurat NYYAZOW died in December 2006, and Turkmenistan held its first multi-candidate presidential election in February 2007. Gurbanguly BERDIMUHAMEDOW, a deputy cabinet chairman under NYYAZOW, emerged as the country's new president; he was chosen as president again in February 2012, in an election that the OSCE said lacked the freedoms necessary to create a competitive environment.

Chapter 2: Geography

Location:

Central Asia, bordering the Caspian Sea, between Iran and Kazakhstan

Geographic coordinates:

40 00 N, 60 00 E

Map references:

Asia

Area:

total: 488,100 sq km

country comparison to the world: 53

land: 469,930 sq km

water: 18,170 sq km

Area - comparative:

slightly larger than California

Land boundaries:

total: 3,736 km

border countries: Afghanistan 744 km, Iran 992 km, Kazakhstan 379 km, Uzbekistan 1,621 km

Coastline:

0 km; note - Turkmenistan borders the Caspian Sea (1,768 km)

Maritime claims:

none (landlocked)

Climate:

subtropical desert

Terrain:

flat-to-rolling sandy desert with dunes rising to mountains in the south; low mountains along border with Iran; borders Caspian Sea in west

Elevation extremes:

lowest point: Vpadina Akchanaya – 81 m

note: Sarygamysh Koli is a lake in northern Turkmenistan with a water level that fluctuates above and below the elevation of Vpadina Akchanaya (the lake has dropped as low as -110 m)

highest point: Gora Ayribaba 3,139 m

Natural resources:

petroleum, natural gas, sulfur, salt

Land use:

arable land: 3.89%

permanent crops: 0.12%

other: 95.98% (2011)

Irrigated land:

19,910 sq km (2006)

Total renewable water resources:

24.77 cu km (2011)

Freshwater withdrawal (domestic/industrial/agricultural):

total: 27.95 cu km/yr (3%/3%/94%)

per capita: 5,752 cu m/yr (2004)

Natural hazards:

NA

Environment - current issues:

contamination of soil and groundwater with agricultural chemicals, pesticides; salination, water logging of soil due to poor irrigation methods; Caspian Sea pollution; diversion of a large share of the flow of the Amu Darya into irrigation contributes to that river's inability to replenish the Aral Sea; desertification

Environment - international agreements:

party to: Biodiversity, Climate Change, Climate Change-Kyoto Protocol, Desertification, Hazardous Wastes, Ozone Layer Protection

signed, but not ratified: none of the selected agreements

Geography - note:

landlocked; the western and central low-lying desolate portions of the country make up the great Garagum (Kara-Kum) desert, which occupies over 80% of the country; eastern part is plateau

Chapter 3: People and Society

Nationality:

noun: Turkmen(s)

adjective: Turkmen

Ethnic groups:

Turkmen 85%, Uzbek 5%, Russian 4%, other 6% (2003)

Languages:

Ukrainian (official) 67%, Russian 24%, other (includes small Romanian-, Polish-, and Hungarian-speaking minorities) 9%

Religions:

Muslim 89%, Eastern Orthodox 9%, unknown 2%

Population:

5,171,943 (July 2014 est.)

country comparison to the world: 120

Age structure:

0-14 years: 26.4% (male 691,076/female 673,310)

15-24 years: 20.2% (male 526,027/female 519,474)

25-54 years: 42.3% (male 1,082,821/female 1,102,716)

55-64 years: 4.2% (male 168,543/female 188,742)

65 years and over: 4.2% (male 95,391/female 123,843) (2014 est.)

Median age:

total: 26.6 years

male: 26.2 years

female: 27.1 years (2014 est.)

Population growth rate:

1.14% (2014 est.)

country comparison to the world: 104

Birth rate:

19.46 births/1,000 population (2014 est.)

country comparison to the world: 89

Death rate:

6.16 deaths/1,000 population (2014 est.)

country comparison to the world: 161

Net migration rate:

-1.86 migrant(s)/1,000 population (2014 est.)

country comparison to the world: 164

Urbanization:

urban population: 48.7% of total population (2011)

rate of urbanization: 1.91% annual rate of change (2010-15 est.)

Major cities - population:

ASHGABAT (capital) 637,000 (2009)

Sex ratio:

at birth: 1.05 male(s)/female

under 15 years: 1.03 male(s)/female

15-24 years: 1.01 male(s)/female

25-54 years: 0.98 male(s)/female

55-64 years: 0.98 male(s)/female

65 years and over: 0.77 male(s)/female

total population: 0.98 male(s)/female (2014 est.)

Maternal mortality rate:

67 deaths/100,000 live births (2010)

country comparison to the world: 90

Infant mortality rate:

total: 38.13 deaths/1,000 live births

country comparison to the world: 60

male: 45.63 deaths/1,000 live births

female: 30.26 deaths/1,000 live births (2014 est.)

Life expectancy at birth:

total population: 69.47 years

country comparison to the world: 155

male: 66.48 years

female: 72.61 years (2014 est.)

Total fertility rate:

2.1 children born/woman (2014 est.)

country comparison to the world: 108

Health expenditures:

2.7% of GDP (2011)

country comparison to the world: 183

Physicians density:

2.44 physicians/1,000 population (2007)

Hospital bed density:

4.1 beds/1,000 population (2011)

Sanitation facility access:

improved:

urban: 100% of population

rural: 98.2% of population

total: 99.1% of population

unimproved:

urban: 0% of population

rural: 1.8% of population

total: 0.9% of population (2011 est.)

HIV/AIDS - adult prevalence rate:

less than 0.1% (2012)

country comparison to the world: 149

HIV/AIDS - people living with HIV/AIDS:

fewer than 200 (2012)

country comparison to the world: 164

HIV/AIDS - deaths:

fewer than 100 (2012)

country comparison to the world: 141

Children under the age of 5 years underweight:

10.5% (2000)

country comparison to the world: 68

Education expenditures:

NA

Literacy:

definition: age 15 and over can read and write

total population: 99.6%

male: 99.7%

female: 99.5% (2011 est.)

Chapter 4: Government and Key Leaders

Country name:

> conventional long form: none
>
> conventional short form: Turkmenistan
>
> local long form: none
>
> local short form: Turkmenistan
>
> former: Turkmen Soviet Socialist Republic

Government type:

> defines itself as a secular democracy and a presidential republic; in actuality displays
> authoritarian presidential rule, with power concentrated within the presidential administration

Capital:

> name: Ashgabat (Ashkhabad)
>
> geographic coordinates: 37 57 N, 58 23 E
>
> time difference: UTC+5 (10 hours ahead of Washington, DC during Standard Time)

Administrative divisions:

> 5 provinces (welayatlar, singular - welayat) and 1 independent city*: Ahal Welayaty (Anew),
> Ashgabat*, Balkan Welayaty (Balkanabat), Dashoguz Welayaty, Lebap Welayaty (Turkmenabat),
> Mary Welayaty
>
> note: administrative divisions have the same names as their administrative centers (exceptions
> have the administrative center name following in parentheses)

Independence:

> 27 October 1991 (from the Soviet Union)

National holiday:

> Independence Day, 27 October (1991)

Constitution:

> adopted 18 May 1992; amended several times, last in 2008; note - sources disagree on whether
> the changes in 2008 are amendments or reflect a new constitution (2012)

Legal system:

> civil law system with Islamic law influences

International law organization participation:

> has not submitted an ICJ jurisdiction declaration; non-party state to the ICCt

Suffrage:

> 18 years of age; universal

Executive branch:

chief of state: President Gurbanguly BERDIMUHAMEDOW (since 14 February 2007); note - the president is both the chief of state and head of government

head of government: President Gurbanguly BERDIMUHAMEDOW (since 14 February 2007)

cabinet: Cabinet of Ministers appointed by the president

elections: president elected by popular vote for a five-year term (eligible for a second term; election last held on 12 February 2012 (next to be held February 2017)

election results: Gurbanguly BERDIMUHAMEDOW reelected president; percent of vote - Gurbanguly BERDIMUHAMEDOW 97.1%, Annageldi YAZMYRADOW 1.1%, other candidates 1.8%

Legislative branch:

unicameral parliament known as the National Assembly (Mejlis) (125 seats; members elected by popular vote to serve five-year terms)

elections: last held on 15 December 2013 (next to be held in December 2018)

election results: percent of vote by party - NA; seats by party - Democratic Party 47, Organization of Trade and Unions of Turkmenistan 33, Women's Union of Turkmenistan 16, Party of Industrialists and Entrepreneurs 14

note: in 26 September 2008, a new constitution of Turkmenistan abolished a second, 2,507-member legislative body known as the People's Council and expanded the number of deputies in the National Assembly from 65 to 125; the powers formerly held by the People's Council were divided up between the president and the National Assembly

Judicial branch:

highest court(s): Supreme Court of Turkmenistan (consists of the court president and 21 associate judges)

judge selection and term of office: judges appointed by the president; judge tenure NA

subordinate courts: provincial, district, and city courts; High Commercial Court; military courts

Political parties and leaders:

Democratic Party of Turkmenistan or DPT [Kasymguly BABAYEW]

Party of Industrialists and Entrepreneurs or PIE [Orazmammet MAMMEDOW] (party registered 21 August 2012)

note: a law authorizing the registration of political parties went into effect in January 2012; unofficial, small opposition movements exist abroad; the three most prominent opposition groups-in-exile are the National Democratic Movement of Turkmenistan (NDMT), the Republican Party of Turkmenistan, and the Watan (Fatherland) Party; the NDMT was led by former Foreign Minister Boris SHIKHMURADOV until his arrest and imprisonment in the wake of the 25 November 2002 attack on President NYYAZOW's motorcade

Political pressure groups and leaders:

International organization participation:

ADB, CIS (associate member, has not ratified the 1993 CIS charter although it participates in meetings and held the chairmanship of the CIS in 2012), EAPC, EBRD, ECO, FAO, G-77, IBRD, ICAO, ICRM, IDA, IDB, IFC, IFRCS, ILO, IMF, IMO, Interpol, IOC, IOM (observer), ISO (correspondent), ITU, MIGA, NAM, OIC, OPCW, OSCE, PFP, UN, UNCTAD, UNESCO, UNHCR, UNIDO, UNWTO, UPU, WCO, WFTU (NGOs), WHO, WIPO, WMO

Diplomatic representation in the US:

chief of mission: Ambassador Mered Bairamovich ORAZOW (since 14 February 2001)

chancery: 2207 Massachusetts Avenue NW, Washington, DC 20008

telephone: [1] (202) 588-1500

FAX: [1] (202) 280-1003

Diplomatic representation from the US:

chief of mission: Ambassador Robert E. PATTERSON (since 26 April 2011)

embassy: No. 9 1984 Street (formerly Pushkin Street), Ashgabat, Turkmenistan 744000

mailing address: 7070 Ashgabat Place, Washington, DC 20521-7070

telephone: [993] (12) 94-00-45

FAX: [993] (12) 94-26-14

Key Leaders:

Pres.
Gurbanguly BERDIMUHAMEDOW

Dep. Chmn. of the Cabinet of Ministers for Agriculture &Water Resources
Annageldi YAZMYRADOW

Dep. Chmn. of the Cabinet of Ministers for Construction
Samuhammet DURDYLYYEW

Dep. Chmn. of the Cabinet of Ministers for Economy &Finance
Annamuhammet GOCYYEW

Dep. Chmn. of the Cabinet of Ministers for Education, Health,Science, Religious Affairs, & Tourism
Sapardurdy TOYLYYEW

Dep. Chmn. of the Cabinet of Ministers for Energy & Industry
Rozymyrat SEYITGULYYEW

Dep. Chmn. of the Cabinet of Ministers for Industry, TurkmenCarpets, Chemicals, Fisheries, & Textiles
Babanyyaz ITALMAZOW

Dep. Chmn. of the Cabinet of Ministers for Intl. Relations
Rasit MEREDOW

Dep. Chmn. of the Cabinet of Ministers for Media & Culture
Byagul NURMYRADOWA

Dep. Chmn. of the Cabinet of Ministers for Oil & Gas
Baymyrat HOJAMUHAMMEDOW

Dep. Chmn. of the Cabinet of Ministers for Trade, Commerce,Textiles, & Customs (Acting)
Palwan TAGANOW

Dep. Chmn. of the Cabinet of Ministers for Transport &Communication (Acting)
Saltyk SALTYKOW

Min. of Agriculture
Rejep BAZAROW

Min. of Communication
Batyr ERESOW

Min. of Construction
Jumageldi BAYRAMOW

Min. of Culture
Gunca MAMMEDOWA

Min. of Defense
Begenc GUNDOGDYYEW

Min. of Economics & Development
Babamyrat TAGANOW

Min. of Education
Gulsat MAMMEDOWA

Min. of Energy
Myrat ARTYKOW

Min. of Environmental Protection
Babageldi ANNABAYRAMOW

Min. of Finance
Dowletgeldi SADYKOW

Min. of Foreign Affairs
Rasit MEREDOW

Min. of Health & Medical Industry
Nurmuhammet AMANNEPESOW

Min. of Internal Affairs
Isgender MULIKOW

Min. of Justice
Begmyrat MUHAMMEDOW

Min. of Labor & Social Protection
Bekmyrat SAMYRADOW

Min. of National Security
Yaylym BERDIYEW

Min. of Oil & Gas Industry & Mineral Resources (Acting)
Muhammetnur HALYLOW

Min. of Public Works Management & Sanitation (Acting)
Atamyrat REJEPOW

Min. of Railways
Bayram ANNAMEREDOW

Min. of Road Transport
Mele GURBANDURDYYEW

Min. of Textile Industry
Saparmyrat BATYROW

Min. of Trade & Foreign Economic Relations
Batyr ABAYEW

Min. of Water Resources
Seyitmyrat TAGANOW

Dir., State Agency for the Management & Use of Hydrocarbon Resources
Yagsygeldi KAKAYEW

Head, State Concern for Turkmen Roads
Asyr SARYBAYEW

Prosecutor Gen.
Amanmyrat HALLYYEW

Chmn., Central Bank
Tuwakmammet JAPAROW

Ambassador to the US
Mered ORAZOW

Permanent Representative to the UN, New York
Aksoltan ATAYEWA

Flag description:

green field with a vertical red stripe near the hoist side, containing five tribal guls (designs used in producing carpets) stacked above two crossed olive branches; five white stars and a white crescent moon appear in the upper corner of the field just to the fly side of the red stripe; the green color and crescent moon represent Islam; the five stars symbolize the regions or welayats of Turkmenistan; the guls reflect the national identity of Turkmenistan where carpet-making has long been a part of traditional nomadic life

note: the flag of Turkmenistan is the most intricate of all national flags

National symbol(s):

Akhal-Teke horse

National anthem:

name: "Garassyz, Bitarap Turkmenistanyn" (Independent, Neutral, Turkmenistan State Anthem)
lyrics/music: collective/Veli MUKHATOV
note: adopted 1997, lyrics revised 2008; following the death of the President Saparmurat NYYAZOW, the lyrics were altered to eliminate references to the former president

Chapter 5: Economy

Economy - overview:

Turkmenistan is largely a desert country with intensive agriculture in irrigated oases and sizeable gas and oil resources. The two largest crops are cotton, most of which is produced for export, and wheat, which is domestically consumed. Although agriculture accounts for roughly 7% of GDP, it continues to employ nearly half of the country's workforce. Turkmenistan's authoritarian regime has taken a cautious approach to economic reform, hoping to use gas and cotton export revenues to sustain its inefficient and highly corrupt economy. Privatization goals remain limited. From 1998-2005, Turkmenistan suffered from the continued lack of adequate export routes for natural gas and from obligations on extensive short-term external debt. At the same time, however, total exports rose by an average of roughly 15% per year from 2003-08, largely because of higher international oil and gas prices. Additional pipelines to China, that began operation in early 2010, and increased pipeline capacity to Iran, have expanded Turkmenistan's export routes for its gas. Overall prospects in the near future are discouraging because of endemic corruption, a poor educational system, government misuse of oil and gas revenues, and Ashgabat's reluctance to adopt market-oriented reforms. The majority of Turkmenistan's economic statistics are state secrets. The present government established a State Agency for Statistics, but GDP numbers and other publicized figures are subject to wide margins of error. In particular, the rate of GDP growth is uncertain. Since his election, President BERDIMUHAMEDOW unified the country's dual currency exchange rate, ordered the redenomination of the manat, reduced state subsidies for gasoline, and initiated development of a special tourism zone on the Caspian Sea. Although foreign investment is encouraged, and some improvements in macroeconomic policy have been made, numerous bureaucratic obstacles impede international business activity.

GDP (purchasing power parity):

$55.16 billion (2013 est.)

country comparison to the world: 95

$49.18 billion (2012 est.)

$44.27 billion (2011 est.)

note: data are in 2013 US dollars

GDP (official exchange rate):

$40.56 billion (2013 est.)

GDP - real growth rate:

12.2% (2013 est.)

11.1% (2012 est.)

14.7% (2011 est.)

GDP - per capita (PPP):

$9,700 (2013 est.)

country comparison to the world: 122

$8,800 (2012 est.)

$8,000 (2011 est.)

note: data are in 2013 US dollars

GDP - composition by sector:

agriculture: 7.2%

industry: 24.4%

services: 68.4% (2013 est.)

Labor force:

2.3 million (2008 est.)

country comparison to the world: 117

Labor force - by occupation:

agriculture: 48.2%

industry: 14%

services: 37.8% (2004 est.)

Unemployment rate:

60% (2004 est.)

country comparison to the world: 199

Population below poverty line:

30% (2004 est.)

Budget:

revenues: $5.93 billion

expenditures: $5.474 billion (2013 est.)

Taxes and other revenues:

14.6% of GDP (2013 est.)

country comparison to the world: 194

Budget surplus (+) or deficit (-):

1.1% of GDP (2013 est.)

country comparison to the world: 24

Inflation rate (consumer prices):

9% (2013 est.)

country comparison to the world: 203

8.5% (2012 est.)

Stock of narrow money:

$577.2 million (31 December 2013 est.)

country comparison to the world: 158

$526.3 million (31 December 2012 est.)

Stock of broad money:

$1.199 billion (31 December 2013 est.)

country comparison to the world: 163

$1.058 billion (31 December 2012 est.)

Stock of domestic credit:

$2.912 billion (31 December 2013 est.)

country comparison to the world: 126

$2.561 billion (31 December 2012 est.)

Current account balance:

$285.9 million (2013 est.)

country comparison to the world: 54

$622.7 million (2012 est.)

Exports:

$17.13 billion (2013 est.)

country comparison to the world: 75

$15.48 billion (2012 est.)

Exports - commodities:

gas, crude oil, petrochemicals, textiles, cotton fiber

Exports - partners:

China 69.6%, Italy 4.7% (2012)

Imports:

$12.48 billion (2013 est.)

country comparison to the world: 92

$10.69 billion (2012 est.)

Imports - commodities:

machinery and equipment, chemicals, foodstuffs

Imports - partners:

China 19.5%, Turkey 17%, Russia 12.6%, UAE 6.8%, Ukraine 6%, Germany 4.7%, UK 4.2% (2012)

Reserves of foreign exchange and gold:

$22.35 billion (31 December 2013 est.)

country comparison to the world: 56

$20.71 billion (31 December 2012 est.)

Debt - external:

$428.9 million (31 December 2012 est.)

country comparison to the world: 179

$451.5 million (31 December 2011 est.)

Exchange rates:

Turkmen manat (TMM) per US dollar -

2.85 (2013 est.)

2.85 (2012 est.)

2.85 (2010 est.)

2.85 (2009)

14,250 (2008)

Fiscal year:

calendar year

Chapter 6: Energy

Electricity - production:

15.66 billion kWh (2010 est.)

country comparison to the world: 80

Electricity - consumption:

11.12 billion kWh (2010 est.)

country comparison to the world: 86

Electricity - exports:

2.41 billion kWh (2010 est.)

country comparison to the world: 39

Electricity - imports:

0 kWh (2012 est.)

country comparison to the world: 144

Electricity - installed generating capacity:

2.852 million kW (2010 est.)

country comparison to the world: 89

Electricity - from fossil fuels:

100% of total installed capacity (2010 est.)

country comparison to the world: 38

Electricity - from nuclear fuels:

0% of total installed capacity (2010 est.)

country comparison to the world: 192

Electricity - from hydroelectric plants:

0% of total installed capacity (2010 est.)

country comparison to the world: 205

Electricity - from other renewable sources:

0% of total installed capacity (2010 est.)

country comparison to the world: 131

Crude oil - production:

244,100 bbl/day (2012 est.)

country comparison to the world: 36

Crude oil - exports:

67,000 bbl/day (2012 est.)

country comparison to the world: 44

Crude oil - imports:

0 bbl/day (2010 est.)

country comparison to the world: 131

Crude oil - proved reserves:

600 million bbl (1 January 2013 est.)

country comparison to the world: 46

Refined petroleum products - production:

143,200 bbl/day (2010 est.)

country comparison to the world: 64

Refined petroleum products - consumption:

145,000 bbl/day (2011 est.)

country comparison to the world: 68

Refined petroleum products - exports:

64,360 bbl/day (2010 est.)

country comparison to the world: 57

Refined petroleum products - imports:

2,542 bbl/day (2010 est.)

country comparison to the world: 176

Natural gas - production:

59.5 billion cu m (2011 est.)

country comparison to the world: 16

Natural gas - consumption:

25 billion cu m (2011 est.)

country comparison to the world: 32

Natural gas - exports:

46.1 billion cu m (2011 est.)

country comparison to the world: 8

Natural gas - imports:

0 cu m (2011 est.)

country comparison to the world: 139

Natural gas - proved reserves:

7.504 trillion cu m (1 January 2013 est.)

country comparison to the world: 6

Carbon dioxide emissions from consumption of energy:

51.85 million Mt (2011 est.)

country comparison to the world: 63

Chapter 7: Communications

Telephones - main lines in use:

575,000 (2012)

country comparison to the world: 94

Telephones - mobile cellular:

3.953 million (2012)

country comparison to the world: 123

Telephone system:

general assessment: telecommunications network remains underdeveloped and progress toward improvement is slow; strict government control and censorship inhibits liberalization and modernization

domestic: Turkmentelekom, in cooperation with foreign partners, has installed high-speed fiber-optic lines and has upgraded most of the country's telephone exchanges and switching centers with new digital technology; combined fixed-line and mobile teledensity is about 80 per 100 persons; Russia's Mobile Telesystems, the only foreign mobile-cellular service provider in Turkmenistan, had its operating license suspended in December 2010 but was able to resume operations in September 2012; Turkmenistan's first telecommunication satellite is scheduled to be launched by the end of 2014; once in orbit, it is expected that the satellite will greatly improve connectivity in the country

international: country code - 993; linked by fiber-optic cable and microwave radio relay to other CIS republics and to other countries by leased connections to the Moscow international gateway switch; an exchange in Ashgabat switches international traffic through Turkey via Intelsat; satellite earth stations - 1 Orbita and 1 Intelsat (2012)

Broadcast media:

broadcast media is government controlled and censored; 7 state-owned TV and 4 state-owned radio networks; satellite dishes and programming provide an alternative to the state-run media; officials sometimes limit access to satellite TV by removing satellite dishes (2007)

Internet country code:

.tm

Internet hosts:

714 (2012)

country comparison to the world: 176

Internet users:

80,400 (2009)

country comparison to the world: 166

Chapter 8: Transnational Issues

Disputes - international:

cotton monoculture in Uzbekistan and Turkmenistan creates water-sharing difficulties for Amu Darya river states; field demarcation of the boundaries with Kazakhstan commenced in 2005, but Caspian seabed delimitation remains stalled with Azerbaijan, Iran, and Kazakhstan due to Turkmenistan's indecision over how to allocate the sea's waters and seabed; bilateral talks continue with Azerbaijan on dividing the seabed and contested oilfields in the middle of the Caspian

Refugees and internally displaced persons:

Stateless persons: 8,947 (2012)

Trafficking in persons:

current situation: Turkmenistan is a source, and to a much lesser degree, destination country for men, women, and children subjected to forced labor and sex trafficking; Turkmen in search of work in other countries are forced to work in textile sweatshops, construction, and domestic service; some Turkmen women and girls are sex trafficked abroad; Turkey is the primary trafficking destination, followed by Russia, the United Arab Emirates, and, to a lesser extent, the UK, Kazakhstan, and Cyprus; labor trafficking occurs within Turkmenistan, particularly in the construction industry, with victims identified from Uzbekistan, Ukraine, and Azerbaijan

tier rating: Tier 2 Watch List - Turkmenistan does not fully comply with the minimum standards for the elimination of trafficking; however, it is making significant efforts to do so; the government continues to convict trafficking offenders under its anti-trafficking statute; it employs no formal victim identification procedures and does not provide services or fund NGOs to provide services to victims; authorities punish some victims for crimes committed as a result of being trafficked; there continues to be no governmental coordinating body for anti-trafficking efforts or a national anti-trafficking action plan (2013)

Illicit drugs:

transit country for Afghan narcotics bound for Russian and Western European markets; transit point for heroin precursor chemicals bound for Afghanistan

Chapter 9: Transportation

Airports:

26 (2013)

country comparison to the world: 126

Airports - with paved runways:

total: 21

over 3,047 m: 1

2,438 to 3,047 m: 9

1,524 to 2,437 m: 9

914 to 1,523 m: 2 (2013)

Airports - with unpaved runways:

total: 5

1,524 to 2,437 m: 1

under 914 m: 4 (2013)

Heliports:

1 (2013)

Pipelines:

gas 7,500 km; oil 1,501 km (2013)

Railways:

total: 2,980 km

country comparison to the world: 57

broad gauge: 2,980 km 1.520-m gauge (2008)

Roadways:

total: 58,592 km

country comparison to the world: 72

paved: 47,577 km

unpaved: 11,015 km (2002)

Waterways:

1,300 km (Amu Darya and Kara Kum canal are important inland waterways) (2011)

country comparison to the world: 56

Merchant marine:

total: 11

country comparison to the world: 112

by type: cargo 4, chemical tanker 1, petroleum tanker 5, refrigerated cargo 1 (2010)

Ports and terminals:

Turkmenbasy

Chapter 10: Military

Military branches:

Turkmen Armed Forces: Ground Forces, Navy, Air and Air Defense Forces (2013)

Military service age and obligation:

18-27 years of age for compulsory male military service; 2-year conscript service obligation, or 1 year for university students; 20 years of age for voluntary service; males may enroll in military schools from age 15 (2013)

Manpower available for military service:

males age 16-49: 1,380,794

females age 16-49: 1,387,211 (2010 est.)

Manpower fit for military service:

males age 16-49: 1,066,649

females age 16-49: 1,185,538 (2010 est.)

Manpower reaching militarily significant age annually:

male: 53,829

female: 52,988 (2010 est.)

Map of Turkmenistan

Other Key Facts™ Titles

All Key Facts™ Titles are Available at www.Amazon.com

THE INTERNATIONALIST®

2013

www.internationalist.com